With love to Doris —

Rod
30 March, 04

ROD McKUEN

Rusting in the Rain

New & Selected Poems

Works by Rod McKuen

BOOKS

Poetry
Stanyan Street & Other Sorrows
Listen to the Warm
Sea Cycle
Lonesome Cities
Revised And Autumn Came
In Someone's Shadow
Twelve Years of Christmas
Caught in the Quiet
Fields of Wonder
With Love
And to Each Season . . .
Come to Me in Silence
Moment to Moment
Seasons in the Sun
Moment to Moment, 2nd Revision
Celebrations of the Heart
Beyond the Boardwalk
Alone
Hand in Hand
The Sea Around Me
Coming Close to the Earth
We Touch the Sky
Love's Been Good to Me
The Power Bright & Shining
Looking for a Friend
The Beautiful Strangers
Too Many Midnights
The Sound of Solitude
Watch for the Wind
Suspension Bridge
Intervals
Valentines
A Safe Place to Land
Rusting in the Rain

Collected Poems & Lyrics
Frank Sinatra: A Man Alone
The Carols of Christmas
The Rod McKuen Omnibus
New Ballads
Grand Tour
Australian Omnibus

Prose
Finding My Father
An Outstretched Hand
A Book of Days
A Book of Days, 2
Another Beautiful Day, I
Another Beautiful Day, II
The Will to Win

Songbooks
New Carols for Christmas
Sinatra Sings McKuen
New Ballads
Sold Out at Carnegie Hall
28 Greatest Hits
Kaleidoscope
A Boy Named Charlie Brown
Joanna
Love's Been Good to Me
Through European Windows
Songs of Rod McKuen, Vol. 1
Songs of Rod McKuen, Vol. 2
19 New Rod McKuen Songs
23 Rod McKuen Songs
The Sea (with Anita Kerr)
Brel/McKuen Songbook
New Johnny Mercer / Rod McKuen Songs (2004)

CLASSICAL WORKS

Concertos
- •For Piano & Orchestra
- For Cello & Orchestra
- For Guitar & Orchestra
- #2 for Piano & Orchestra
- For Four Harpsichords
- For Ondes Martenot & Orchestra

Symphonies, Symphonic Suites, Etc.
- Symphony No. 1
- •Ballad of Distances
- •The City, for Narrator & Orchestra
- •I Hear America Singing (to the poetry of Walt Whitman)
- Piano & String Suites
- Adagio for Harp & Strings
- Rigadoon for Orchestra
- •Birch Trees: For Piano & Strings
- Seascapes for Piano
- Pastures Green
- •Symphony No. 2
- •Symphony No. 3, Opus 42
- Symphony No. 4
- The Art of Catching Trains
- Variation for Piano and Orchestra

Chamber
- Piano Sonatas
- Concerto for Four Hands
- Piano Trios
- Piano Quartets
- Sonata for Ondes Martenot
- Octet for 4 French Horns
- Serenade for Trombone

Ballet
- Americana R.F.D.
- •Point/Counterpoint
- Elizabethan Dances
- The Minotaur (Man to Himself)
- Volga Song
- Full Circle
- •The Plains of My Country
- Man Who Tracked Stars
- •Americana RFD
- •Something Beyond
- •Written in the Stars

Opera & Vocal Music
- The Black Eagle
- Seven Cynical Songs
- Nebraska Sonnets
- Home by Water (music by Eric Sate)
- Things to Come (music by Eric Sate)
- •The Wind of Change (music by J. Rodrigo)
- Inside of Me (music by J. Rodrigo)
- •Silver Apples of the Moon

Major Film Scores
- The Prime of Miss Jean Brodie
- Joanna
- Emily
- Scandalous John
- A Boy Named Charlie Brown (in collaboration)
- Me Natalie (in collaboration)

Television Scores
- Travels with Charley
- The Unknown War
- The Borrowers
- Lisa Bright and Dark
- The Beach
- Imaginary Landscapes
- Come to Your Senses
- Matinee Theatre
- Manhattan

• Denotes commissions

ROD McKUEN

Rusting in the Rain

New & Selected Poems

A CHEVAL / STANYAN BOOK

Published by the Stanyan Music Group
Box 2783 • Hollywood CA 90028 • USA
www.stanyanhouse.com

RUSTING IN THE RAIN. Copyright © 2004 by Rod McKuen and The Stanyan Music Group. All rights reserved. Printed in the United States of America. No part of this book may be used, recorded, or reproduced in any form or manner whatsoever without written permission except in the case of brief quotations embodied in critical articles and reviews.

Some of this material first appeared in the quarterly FOLIO and on the Web site A Safe Place to Land. For a complete list of sources & additional copyrights see Source listing.

FIRST EDITION • January 2004

10 9 8 7 6 5 4 3 2 1

Library of Congress Cataloging-in-Publication Data

McKuen, Rod.
A Safe Place to Land

ISBN # 0-910368=05=8

Rod McKuen's Website A Safe Place to Land is located on the Internet at www. rodmckuen.com & www.mckuen.com

For Edward

Contents

SUMMERTREE 13
- Summertree 15
- And Yet 18
- Overhead The Clouds 20
- Holding On 21
- Mathematics 23
- Nobody's Heart 25
- Nostalgia 27
- Summertree, Two 29

ARMFULLS OF AUGUSTS 33
- Some Things 35
- August Asks for Little 38
- At Leisure 41
- Sacrament 42
- Music Room 45
- Sandbag 47
- August Moon: Maui · 2003 48
- The Moon as a Mirage 50
- Mid August 51
- Through the Field 53

IF LOVE WERE ALL 55
- Beach Bar Lingo 57
- Noon 58
- After Hours Acrobatics 59
- The Truthful Lover 61
- To One Absent 63
- Taking Leave 64

        When Valentines are Obsolete 65
        After Love 66
        Night Mischief 68
        Always Beginning 70

THE MYSTIC WARRIER 71
        Imaginary Friendships 73
        In Certain Cities 75
        Warren's Warren 76
        Looking for a Friend 78

SEASONED CITIZENS 81
        Winter People 83
        Lillian at Fifty 86
        Can We Have Our Ball Back 87
        Daylily Blossoms 90
        Roundabout 91
        A Crock of Flowers 92

DOWNLOADING THE CLASSICS 93
        Some Sopranos 95
        Castrati 98
        Madame Butterfly 99
        La Boheme 100
        Carmen 101
        Ludwig Answers his Critics 102

AMERICAN STRAND 103
        American Strand 105
        Courage 107
        Reality 108
        Riders to the Stars 109

    Iowa from Above 110

THAT WAS THEN 113
    Elko Winter, 1946 115
    San Francisco, 1953 117
    Tagu Korea 1955 118
    The Yellow Unicorn, 1959 120
    The Coming of the Rain, 1967 123
    From a Moscow Notebook, April 1978 125
    That Was Then 130

THIS IS NOW 133
    This is Now 135
    Still Life After all These Years 137
    I Always Knew 141
    The Poet Caught Mid Song 145

A BETTER PLACE 151
    The Possible 153
    High Heavens There Are 155
    Don't Imagine Endings 156
    Circles & Squares 158
    Earthling 159
    A Few of Us Will Still Stay On 162
    Caveat 163

Index to First Lines 165
About the Author 167
About the Production of This Book 170
Additional Sources 171

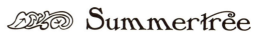 Summertree

for Ken Blackie

Summertree

for Scott Savole

He had hoped that even as an older tree
in need of other tree limbs to caress,
caressing his and enter twining with them,
a sapling strong and true might in time
                        sprout up close enough
to his weathered trunk
to make a reach, toward him if only
                        for a tickle or a touch.

Hey, Old Feller, it might say,
Awake, awake and smell the morning clover
nibbling at your ground pushed roots. Look
and see that young bird of such focused industry
refurbishing a nest amid your bulging branches.
Up there in your lofty limbs you'll have
                        a set of heavy squeakers soon.

Not much chance of that. Young saplings
go in search of others of their kind. Alas,
that is as it is, always was and should be.
How else to make a grove from plantlets
                        dispersed and seeking?

And why on such a long and languid, lolling about
pre-summer day should he be sighing for
                           young sprout's attention?
He had weathered lightning, everything.

Trees grow where the rivers run
unless they happen to be ancient Oaks
who long ago tapped deep down springs
for richer rivers sustenance.

He saw a line of stately Poplars
along a distancing horizon, my, he thought,
they make an elegant, imposing sight. So strong,
so straight, so skyward headed. Such friends
they must be to one another Caresses,
even from a wind that causes branch of one
to brush another's branch, must finally become
                           redundant, unnecessary.

After a time one Oak in a field alone
will go unnoticed, not threatening or even strange.
The world moves on to other curiosities
Initials long ago carved delicate but deep upon
An old Oak's trunk gives way to barks renewal.

Children who had once made rope and rubber tire
swings to hang upon its lower limb pass into history,
as do schools and distant belching factory.

Say, that bird up there is really going at it.

Fresh cries and chirps will certainly be welcome
                              when and if they come.

But can I wait, he mused. The loneliness of evening's
like an itch that only branch from other tree
                              could scratch.

And Yet

Love winds down
as does the day, life too
at some unexpected moment.
We do not anticipate any of it.

Love could have, should have, given us
         a few more precious moments.
The day is never long enough.
Too few hours, much left undone.
And life? Who but a fool wants to
                        let go of it?
And yet,
you cannot, dare not,
take love beyond its chosen,
                natural course.

Without night
what asylum would we have from the rigor
of the day. Life, my life, yours, insignificant
to anyone but us.

The universe revolved,
evolved, without us and will go on turning
when we are rust and dust and gone.

You come back to me,
         horizon to horizon,
the stars do not inhibit your return.
Your face framed by the filigree
                of fireflies

or the suns' undoing is still your face.
It needs no elaboration to be more
than what it is. A face, what I prize
above all else, unless it is the rest of you
validating all of me.

And yet,
I do forget you
at odd times, conjuring
is no substitute for things conjugal.
Away I worry that your loved smile,
tolerated frown, will fade from memory
the way a paid off debt does. That is
because I depend on the reality of you
more than I trust my own imagination.

As each dawn's edge
slips away unable to return
and we make light of it or worse,
              note not it's passing,
morning is little more than the end
of night. So much of what we do and
are is made of mere perception,
the rim of anything is mere whim
and not much more.

And yet,

Overhead the Clouds

The space between us now
is greater than
        the space around us.
The walls a little higher,
the window through to you
a little farther up above my head
                and narrow,
narrow to the view.

Options and alternatives
have been replaced by either/or.
Under feet the unmown grass
        mourns low.

In the street dead leaves
        are stirring,
overhead the clouds move faster.

Go along. I'm sorry but I can't keep up.

Holding On

I am content to count
the cobblestones and bricks
    of backyard walks.

Like the inchworm in the half step,
I re-examine soil surveyed
    and leaf already tagged.
The arteries' arithmetic
        will not be stopped.

I wait. I await. The heart
holds on. I am being true
to life as I have known it.

And life is never absolute,
it runs on chicken feet
    between God's wink
and the Devil's asshole.
Somewhere in that distance
love is found or finds us.

What matters is the quality
of solitude we keep
while waiting to be found
    or found out,
thought up or thought about.
Solitude is never sure.

It has no seamark
without excursion into piety
    and disbelief.
As one end confirms the other
so too the move from silence
to the subway grunt.

The rattle underneath the street
proves the worth of silence.

Mathematics

Dawn is the decider. Not just of night
and morning, light that pushes darkness
from horizon to horizon or even
the end of night in favor of the day.
It is the separator of dreams. The
creeper, like a vine, that crawls through
cracks and gaping holes where emptiness
has long been stronghold.

It will not be crowded out in favor of
reality. It forces us to think, commands
us back into whatever world we tried
escaping from by embracing blackness.

Dreams do not die easily or double up
and fall from off the night's edge,
They stay on.

Dividers only separate what already is.
We cannot multiply, subtract or add
unless some substance sits in waiting.

Dawn has never knowingly or with
a touch of malice slain the daydream.
It is still controlled by each of us,
subject only to the living out or lost by
ill attention, laziness or what we term
forgetting. In truth we do give up
on some of our most cherished dreams.
Ah, but never in the night.

Nobody's Heart   for Julie Harris

I am the blade
that slices the rose
from off of its stem
     to the bottle.

I am the table
the chair is tucked under.
I am the engines throttle.

I am the willow
with branch downcast
who never looks up
     at the sparrow.

I am the arrow
aimed at the jugular
that enters the heart of the heart.

I am the woman
who sat by the sea
and swallowed the world
     as she waited.

I am the rock
who hit the king's eye
the first week in October.

I am justice,
a little one-sided,
ashamed to be part
    of the system.

I am the name
that wasn't crossed off
pleased to have been invited.

I am the noun
that wants to be useful.
Why am I not a verb?

I am the valentine
still unopened
that nobody ever sent.

I am the opening
you came through
to get to the other side.

I am the valentine
still unopened
that nobody's heart will ride.

Nostalgia

With the morning's early breath
      I feel you still.
It is as if no quarreling
      and years had come along
           to waltz between us.

When night hovers
and the last slow wind
starts to shudder, shiver,
I smell your hair
as near clear as I inhale
the mustiness of age. It is
the smoke of days and life
             gone by.

In stillness when the rain begins
Its metered military march,
my pulse beat starts its own
dress drill. It is the dust of little
centuries that only now comes
to haunt and not to purify.

When I weary my eyes will well
with sights no longer near -
if they were ever so.

It is the steady blink
of boredom that destroys
imperfect recollections and
the memoirs awaiting confirmation.

Long before the colors fade
                the image goes.

Summertree, two

The old oak stands
              almost alone
as he has stood for ages, eons maybe.
No regrets, recriminations, none.
The strength he's gathered from
              may have been more joyous
and more comforting to live amid the forest
touching branches with his peers, communicating
with the local club of trees and vines. Part of
the great community, mixing in until he blended
blandly with the canopy that guards the moss
and shades the gentle fern and underbrush,
while stunting growth and robbing sunlight
from young saplings, would be trees.

It is the way of neighborhoods and communes
to put self and the like group first. Never mind
that sagging Sycamore across the street.

The Oak had heard Forrest murmurs long ago
and knew, from picked up gossip, rumblings,
passing leaves the wind had carried and even
laughter after lightning, that he was different.

At first he felt isolated, outcast.
But through the years he learned to revel
in this being different, not like others, original,
separate and separated. One of a kind has
its advantages, he often mused, while knowing
there would always be absence of something,
the consequence of non-conformity.

The something missing was the touch, embraces
              from the unknown others.
Some nights he ached as he considered the awful
possibility of only warmth from distant sun
and none from new Oak that would grow nearby
then lean toward him with a promised touch.
Touch is everything to old trees, handshakes
Become embraces, an arm around the shoulder,
near copulation. Mistake rub-up of branch for love?
Not likely, but love from distance or nearby is only
love
while touch grows rarer as the circles round his
trunk
tick off the centuries of even strongest Oak.

The probabilities of stray Wisteria or even
simple ivy groping through the grass toward him
for a climb was too remote to ruminate about.

Ah well, the years alone had all been good to him
and more would come. The Summertree
would nap a bit, then check the progress
of the nest construction in his snowy foliage
later in the afternoon.

If I close my eyes a bit, a dream might happen by.

I imagine, though I would not know for certain,
even old Oaks go on dreaming.

Armfuls of Augusts

Some Things

I never saved your letters,
though I wish I had. Instead
I kept and go on keeping jars
of rocks from beaches now
forgotten and the letter jacket
from a would be athlete friend
who if he had lived would wonder
at and be amazed to think that
someone bothered putting by
a coat he had run inside of
before the runner stumbled.

We do not know what love is
as it passes, as it goes. And that
is why no few of us are always out
collecting other peoples cast off trash.

Who knows what may wind up redeemable
as memory, some stones not flat enough
to skip on water, a jacket with a stain of
blood on the letter H. The heart that was
not once inside the sleeve that wore it
may only wonder and be sad.

Life and love so far removed and yet
so intertwined that one without the other
does not click or work. Can love redeem?
It can. Can love condemn? It can. Can love,
never mind. Whatever the question, it can.

Life, what of it. It is too little until
you realize it is too late.

Of course our minds can and should be
put to better function than mere memory
yet in the end what is collected in our
memory banks are all we are. The past
has made of us what those in the
present see. The future, not just
unsure but unsafe and frightening.

The night outside is ever working but
not always to good purpose. And that
is why you see some of us after nine
o'clock exhorting darkness to bee kind.
Be gentle to all people after closing
hours. It costs you nothing but a nod.

Losing our possessions does not
mean we lose ourselves, but a seashell
in the pocket can be as valuable
as a seashore memory. One triggers
                              the other.

We continue to acquire, accumulate hearts
and habits and stuff of lesser consequence,
rubber bands and pushpins, a penny
in a shoe. Gear that would mean
nothing to some someone else but
matter we as individuals are reluctant
to let go of. Even those odd objects
forgotten in a drawer or saved
in boxes not sorted through
for years define us, are us.

August Asks for Little

I hold in wonderment
the wonders of the day;
the dalliance of daisies in the valley
              just below the hill,
the odor of the earth, my ardor
for you as you lie awake against it.

Above your citron-breasts
the nearly cloudless sky is treated
to that honey mouth I traverse often.

I have learned by heart your soft
            and nearly alabaster belly.
I fall asleep against it
            even when I am away.
Just now my head is upon it and my lips
Are parting to your skin.

As the afternoon glides on love's weight
does not worry us, it conquers the minute,
                  compliments the hour.

August asks for little and is not
                              easily impressed.
If a bright palanquin passed by with heaven
held aloft within it August would only nod.
This lazy month is slow to notice niceties
but it admires the bravery of love.

And now
the night is coupling with the body
                              of the world
and we have moved from hillside
                              to the fire.
For those who lie alone this night, a prayer,
that whomever you are waiting for
comes soon and brings along a pocketful
of stars to scatter in your wake on every
dusky eve like this that looms ahead.

Your love continues to sedate me. My arm
across your shoulder has united us as one.
Crows are crawling through the trees
to nests they made ten years ago.

August asks for little and does not
                              participate.
Whether the wind comes wickedly or with
good intent is of little consequence
to its languid longitude and latitude,
but August lets us be ourselves.

Love is swarming over us
For singing hearts the fairytale
is never over.

At Leisure

I enter you, rest awhile,
        the darkness here is safe.

How I would love to turn the page
of every day in this same way
see everything from your eyes
looking out. Touch what there is
to touch with your fingers, kneading
up against the afternoon as part
of your thighs rubbing.

My cheek grazing yours is like
resolve. The finality of forever.

Your tongue is warm and damp
at leisure in my mouth.
I lounge along your leg
then loaf inside of you.

The only movement anywhere
is the dawn's bright diamond necklace
as it strings itself across horizons new.

Sacrament

I like my body lying next to yours.

I like my leg against your leg
        and over it
the muscle quivering to touch
nothing to obviate the moment.
The luxury of thighs that open onto thighs
is like alighting in a universe you knew
was there but never knew
I like our sighs together and I like
my body lying next to yours at night
            and every morning.

I wear you
coming next to you
as I would clean cotton shirt
soft to the touch you are and tingling.
And everything you border, tap against
is but a punctuation to yourself.

I love the loss of vagrancy inside your arms
your fingers swarming on my back
        like bees attacking single flower.
The light from out your eyelids coming.
The puzzled humming in my ear
as you nod yes not having heard
the question that I asked.

Your hair unmasked for what it is -
a tangled web of craziness
is like a whim not taken up.
So too your mouth is glowing, fair,
runs hot and cold and in no pattern.
I like our elbows, noses, knees
interrupting rhythms that should be truer.

Your breasts are skillful, genius each,
priceless in a bed world
whose currency is chance.

I love the ample of you
        and the lean
the part of you expecting flesh
and rising up to meet it.

The symmetry of you is what I savor
        odd angles too
those energy-propelling sighs
and little cries from you.
The ivory underside of you
the tanned and glowing legs and arms.

I love the winding up of you
as much as the unwinding.
The kindness of your inner ear
is more than I can bear to speak about.

All honey to the heart,
all pasture to the eyes
the size of you is one great breath
taken in, held, not expelled, not ever.
Ingenious are your ankles, calves, hips
Stepping-stones to that great wonder
                    on ahead.

What I love most in all the world
is my own body next to yours.
It is a vanity, a wonderful conceit.

Music Room

The melody begins.
A single note that spreads
    across a harp like night
that doubles back upon itself
growing as I grow along your leg
and then inside you full song.
Your mouth now orchestrates my own,
we soar on music from another sphere
each the other's instrument.
No strings stretched on cherry wood
or calfskin tightened into drums.
                We are only us,
not cellos or the double bass.

I read you with the eagerness
of scholars poring over manuscripts
                    unpublished,
written by composers of another time.
We collaborate.
Where your theme ends and mine begins
                Is now so blurred
neither knows the source of inspiration

I came upon three moles
            like quarter notes,
moving from your lower stomach
            to your inner leg.
I track them with my tongue
and I am led to wet marsh land
where jungle vine and cattail grow.

In this dark sweet-smelling wood
let new language have its start.
Let old arithmetic give way
to older kinds of counting,
not new math but abacus.
Let sleep steal me now
so that I'll awaken
in this self-same place,
to hike again through deeper woods.

Sandbag

Now slowly like a muffled drum
or the rat-a-tat of rain
the beating of your heart
goes back to steadiness.

Silence separates us as our
pulses slow. A rivulet rolls down
between us as though the act
of making love has business hours
and five o'clock has finally come.

I know that love is not
red hearts or flesh on flesh
at pre-set and appointed times
and I believe it to be more
than rhymes and rhyming,
so when I ease to sleep
 against your side
consider my now spent,
sandbag heavy body
as something heart and mind
 let go of
as fodder for a dam
to stop the would be rivulet
now widening to river
from becoming flood.

August Moon: Maui, 2003

No ordinary moons orbit in August.
I know because five dozen round full
melons from that month have followed
me and taken care of me in troubled
times and those when joy went jumping
with me. I was not surprised when the
eighth month Maui moon brought
the real and unexpected you.

The double rainbow of your eyes
and how your back narrows
to such perfect mounds of longing,
the way your neck curves down and
suddenly becomes your shoulders with
no seam between them is a marvel.

Belly to belly when we tangled treasure
trails that merged into a single highway
leading to the haven heaven of your
thighs felt and feels like home.
Lying on my side past midnight I watched
a patch of moonlight track your nipples
to their source and followed it.

This was the century, the month, the August of the year that Mars bent closest to the moon, as we played beneath those planets I felt we were a quartet for the ages.

Whatever and how many Augusts lie ahead none will compare to that sweet month we shared. You against the flame and me inside of it.

Wizardry is to be expected beneath the moons of August but enchantment is no less a wonder whenever it arrives.

The Moon as a Mirage

Buzz saw-like, the full moon now
begins to slice through lower clouds
so steadily and purposeful it must be
             marching to the rhythm
of this moment, yours and mine.

Do not look away or you might miss
its climb across this heaven and its slide
back down the inside of another day.
Moons filling should be savored
                as they swell.

It will do no good to try and summon
this one later in the week. Make,
merry, celebrate its circumference while
it widens in its vaults and acrobatics.
As I grow against you press in close
and take another longer glance over
my shoulder at the rising and the rising
                of the moon.

Mid August

August has been halved.
The warm part done, the cooling
just now starting. If Indian summer
is to be reality it will congregate at
noon and disappear by five -barring
any miracle or as yet a plan set out
but not disclosed.

I light the balcony with candles
just before the sun takes leave
sit outside sweatered,
the phonograph pipes out long,
lean lines of nearly bare baroque.
Crickets count out counterpoint
as though rehearsed and listening.

It seems at times as if each thing
that moves upon the earth
or underneath the sky is trying to
communicate, say something that
needs saying. For now the crickets
add Brazilian beats
to music of another time.

These ancient dancers set the cats
competing for attention. Distracted
by the day's end, caught up
in the night's beginning I ignore their
coaxing for a snuggle or a scratch,
until they turn to cat on cat games.

On this late summer evening we should
be about the manufacture of thoughts
or lack of same. The cats are making
abstract mischief while I get up
to change the music.

Through the Field

I walked home through the field alone
looking at the row on row
          of dead cornstalks
           frightened by the frost
arrested by the first long breath of autumn.
I felt a little older
            but without new knowledge.
Passing through the now past summer
          I have learned nothing.

True, I've memorized your thighs
your burnt brown breasts
        your eyes, your eyes
but you were busy memorizing
             other people's hands
the kindness of their summer crotches
the sounding of their sighs
so without attending your same school
you as pupil and as teacher too
I came into the autumn knowing little new.
Bend to me this first long autumn night
    or let me bend to you.

If Love Were All
for Elaine Stritch

Beach Bar Lingo

Beach bar lingo
being all the same we were left
to make whole conversations
         out of nearly nothing.

Add to this
that glances must be tentative
for none should know our business
         but ourselves.

I wonder that we met at all.
Perhaps the language of the desperate
is the strongest one yet made.

How else could you explain
an understanding without words?
A moving out the door
with no pre-arrangement?

Noon

I watch you
slowly turning gold
beneath this out of season
sun and think how difficult
our life will be together now
that our independent lives
are done. I made a rhyme
without intention. I only meant
to put down for some near
or distant day ahead
you turning brown all over
me turning over in my head
some doubts I've lately
come upon
that rack me for no reason.

After-Hours Acrobatics

I light one candle with another's flame
and getting up to leak I look across at you
still curled and sleeping. Coming back
I start to pass a mirror, I stop. Stand back
and see me naked in the candlelight.

Was I ever beautiful, ever young or wise
deserving of your arms or others'?
Head-on is even harsh by candle glow
love handles bulge on either side
of what was once an unfilled frame
that I hung hopes on, never excess flesh.
My frown attacks my own reflection.
I turn full body, knowing even funhouse
mirrors are kinder than three-quarter views.

A single movement straightens back and
shoulders, tucks a stomach into place.
Not good. Not good enough. This copy
of reality is as sorry as the warped original.

I look at you a second time, hoping I can
dive beneath the covers before you catch
my silhouette against the wall. My pulse
thumps loud enough to blunt ongoing
metronome of cicada calling to cicada.
Safe. I hit third base and slide to home.
You only turn and grumble in your sleep.

I do not drift back to sleep.

All life is spent erecting barricades
that none of us can get through when
                love finally arrives.

The Truthful Lover   for Chen Sam

How fragile are the dreams
                that cross and meet
and make up love.
As need is but a plain name for desire
so too the lies that lovers use in conquest
should be held to light,
cost and consequence not pushed aside.

Whenever love comes calling in the night
                truth bends a little.
That is to be expected.
Love is a non-exclusive instrument.
It is a savings bank,
interest computed and compounded
high above the principal.
It is a place to gather
where lover and beloved
           never come as equals.
And yet the body at its widest
is no wider than the brain that drives it.

Who is the truthful lover,
                    how can we know?
Supposing we pass over that one
who seems like all the rest,
            but only comes by once?

How is Aphrodite now and where is she?
And if she called us each by name
would we discern her voice
in crowded room and reverie?
The questions pile. The answers
run down through the distance
                like a world unwinding.

In love there is no training ground,
only happy accidents.

To One Absent

I do not have to be with you
to have high spirits.
Knowing you are there,
            wherever there is, is enough.
To think of you and know that some
Whenever we will be together always
is all the always that I need just now.
I waited for you all my life, a few days,
years, whatever more is less than all
the decades spent hoping you
would finally come, until you did.

However brief the hours that we
have spent within each other's arms
so far was / is time enough
to see me through this absence of you
                        however long.

Taking Leave

Goodbye is a word that should be
used only to acquaintances or distant
relatives, those who speed away
at bus stops or taxi curbs. Friends
the army carries off and children
heading out to seek their fortune
in towns more fortuitous than
those they leave. It is a word
I will not say to you.

Not on deathbed or in driveway
will you hear my fare thee well.

At the start of some day trip that
separates us sunup till sundown I
might intone so long or hang on
but good-bye? Never.

Remember how reluctantly we
spoke our alohas on telephones
when talking island to continent,
multiply that same reluctance
tenfold when thinking of goodbye.

Hello, I must be going, he says,
wiggling his moustache.

When Valentines are Obsolete

When valentines are obsolete
and love laced letters come no more
will nights be half again as sweet
as those that made our passions soar?

What will survive the hourglass?
A piece of silver string perhaps
to hang upon some ancient tree
initialed once by lovers who
held each others heads in laps
much the same as you and me.

Life will change on passing feet
but love that time defying thing
will always make the heart to beat
and cause the harshest voice to sing.

After Love

Was ever a bed so long awaited
     as the one I come to now?
Did ever a heart anticipate
the regulated beat that comes
when life is straight, alive and true
and no love threatens throb or throes?

Was ever a night so starry as
the one I've just come through?
On nights past did I appreciate
the stars and surplus starlet
satellites gossiping and crowding
skies. All that gleaming, luster talk,
audible to my ears only.

Falling out of love was easier than
I thought it might be, you only had
to turn your back. Age, confronted
by indifference
          can be a magic wand.

I have but a few years and so
much love left, I can ill afford
to waste them on the absent lover.

Was ever a bed so anticipated
as the one I come to now? Empty,
yes, but for the cat. Even the memories,
going, gone. Ah, the thrill of it all.

Night Mischief

A young man standing
in the rain outside that so
         familiar window
known to me because
I have lived across the street
from it too many years, too long.

Known to me because it is unlike
any other window,
and what stays or sits or struts
behind / beyond it is familiar
 if not known to me.

My domain is not my own
not because it is shared,
although it is not but because
he does not share it.
I should have left that first day
I saw him gliding up the stairs.

Or later as I began to notice
others arrive or go beneath
his balcony then up those stairs.

So many coming round the corner
on the sidewalk or the street
over tipping taxi drivers
as they found the right house
and dropped their passenger
four feet from the door.

Just now the door is answered
and another young man
     steps inside.
Outside the rain still falls a mist
embellishes the scene.

Long ago I should have packed
and gone or walked across
the street, smiled and told him
how he was an interruption
in my life, but I was new to this.

Without a no he let me know.

Always Beginning

A health to everything that's new,
the new child just now being born
new lambs in the spring
              new wine in the fall
and those in the years ahead who
come upon each one of us, in the
darkness or the light and find us
new and even necessary.

A health to those of us old enough
to know that newness lives within
the eye and is not measured by
the moonlight or the time of spring
              the poetry in anything.
Newness is a poem of itself
and needs no decoration.

A health to my fat belly and to your
unsteady leg and to those strangers
in the months ahead who will believe
that we are beautiful in spite of or
              because of them.

The Mystic Warrier
for Tom Truhe

Imaginary Friendships   for Larry Baillie

How good it feels to concentrate
on others, foreigners or farmers,
women in the street and those
                within my head.
Lumberjacks and loudmouths.
Mothers chasing children and the child
                making mischief
working at eluding parent.

Lovers courting
squaring off within the dance
then dancing circles round each other
                pairing off.
Exchanging partners or tripping
through the day not as dancers
but as audience to those who love
and live their life loves out before
                the world.

What a time this end of summertime
                to just observe
to call the world my friend
and let imaginary friendships
                tumble in my head.

An old man holding up a wall
I pass by and we are friends.
The muscled runner on a beach
         now here, now gone
but oh there was a longing
in his eyes and gait.
The dog that tags along with
         no one, anyone,
is a friend to me and the less
I imagine him to be loved
the more my friendship for him
grows and stays inside of me

The stranger jostled not by mistake
         inspiring dangerous thoughts
and there are friends I have made
and lost and made again without
their knowledge.

So many leaning on so many
different trees in so many meadow
lands, different leas are sweet August,
         august friends.

In Certain Cities

In certain cities you will find
treasure left behind by those
who went away or got away
just in time from the misery of
                          sameness.

In other towns in other climes
those who were left or stayed
will break your heart with tales
of why and how then could
have turned into a now.

Regrets, recriminations, I have
none, for I am still running.
Over the years my course
has changed. Instead of
going from, I head toward.

Warren's Warren

Tis a good job
Warren does not have a garden.
His disapproving glance toward
a sofa stacked with maps and books,
open & unmarked, can wither furniture,
make couches, even those with comfy
knitted doilies on them, crouch or go away.
A lowering of his disapproving eye causes
scattered papers in an unkempt room
to shrink to corners or to shrivel and
be done; go to compost long before
they would have gone to seed and
glory, according to their season.

And when a bit of love and time
are needed to wait out dusty
picture frames until their silver
linings turn to inch of planting soil
Warren's cleansing eye instead of
Cloroxed lint, wipes surface clean
and indivisible.

All hail the power of his order, and, I guess, his neatness too. But damn his eye that probes the inconsistencies of dust within her stare and questions clutter on her brow that was not there a hundred years ago; the day they met.

Looking for a Friend

If one thousand men
walking through this world room
to room then home again ask for
      your friendship,
know that I am one
within the thousand.

If one hundred men
making do within this world
in city places or the kindest
country fall down fighting for
      your friendship,
know I am on the battlefield
amid the hundred.

If twenty men
who know and knew this world
from crested hills to uncrowned
valley send letters breathing for
      your friendship,
expect my letter soon
among the twenty.

If one man
living in this too-gray world
running crooked roads or pacing
pavements comes in need of
      your friendship
be not amazed or disbelieve,
I am that one man.

If no one
comes to you carrying a New World
in his arms, at his back or in a
wagon offering it for
      your friendship
know that I have been detained
but even now am on my way.

Still no one
Comes to you within this world
when two dozen years or half of
that has passed and you
      feel friendless,
do not come and seek me out
for I'll be lifeless in a grave and gone.

Perhaps you were hiding or
concerned with other, larger things
but know that while I lived
I went on looking.

 Seasoned Citizens

for Theodore Raaf

Winter People

Discarded. Given up. With lifetimes
left to give. Life itself has been
your cloak and classroom now sent away
to live or pretend at living, not students
or the jailer children who shuttled you
to ghettos of neglect come calling.

Now voyager,
I ask you did you do your early traveling
turning from the spinster aunt to Cinderella
                                      for this?

I have seen you in the winter,
sitting on the same long benches, before
you sit, carefully dusting the snow from
off the green of those slatted sitting spots.

No pigeons left to feed. All have made
their winter pilgrimage to Boca or some
such sunny clime.

Old man how old is old? One half of one ear lost
to hearing? A smile that did not come on time
because you felt the need to think before reacting
                              to a not so funny joke?

Old couples, odd as obelisks where is the proof
of your true worth within your children's eyes?

Old friends will still be in the neighborhood
you never wished to leave. Don't depend on visits.
Your new familiars will be families of every kind
appearing once a week on television, not funny
anymore and too young to relate to.

Widows, widowers and those about to be.
Those you gave to have given you up,
but I beg you, don't give up on your own selves.
Write. Wire. Call collect. Anybody. Dial a prayer
or me, radio voices in the night, The President.
                    Well maybe not The President,
high officials as you know are always otherwise
                                        Engaged.

Do not let go especially if there is even one
relative still poised and purring,
                    spoiling to collect the spoils.

Rewrite your will cutting out petition signers and
offspring busy during business hours, business being
anything but you.

Leave your estate to the state, the city or
the country, they were always late but never too
late.

I love the winter people, love them
as the lilacs blooming still amid the snow -
but check me out before you will to me your
lorgnette
or your dusty bible, as a lover, loving when and
where
I can, I love true and truthfully giving over all I own
each time. That would include your legacy.

But never mind, Winter People I have joined your
                    ranks and I find I like it here.

Lillian at Fifty

Snow has now begun to comb her hair,
soft patch of winter at each temple
where only summer grew before.
Her voice thick-throated,
      a murmured whisper in the pines.
And there are lines
      about the corners of her eyes
more beautiful than love words written down
and sent away, Browning-to-Browning.
Her breasts no longer point immodestly -
they bend and coil and fit into her body
curve, the way a lover's arm was meant
to cradle that so-perfect head just found.

From bath to bedroom and to bed.
She is not just that flawless woman
                  in my life
but premier woman of the world,
created wholly by herself,
made up to make a mold for womanhood.
And I, mortal lover of immortality.
What man could dream up heaven better
than she who lets the snow begin
      to softly comb her hair?

Can We Have Our Ball Back

I wish I could give back to you
the first one you had so long ago, the
one that wore out, got mislaid or stolen
or just cast aside because you grew
too old to play ball or play with balls.

The baseball you hit into the wood.
The one you sent to the top of the tent
that rolled down the side and under
the slide and was gone forever.
If ever a ball deserved to boomerang

back it was that one, now gone
that will not be retrieved by what
we believe or believed. The trouble with
balls is the trouble with all those things
left behind is some other time or mindset.

We always forget to forget them
in time to move on, get on with what
ever whatever is. That stuff we gave up
ball games for, forgot all the names for
as we traveled from there to here.

We do not select our memories they
choose us. Why not a ball, an agate,
a sled instead of the boy who went
away, the girl who broke your heart
at eleven. I wish I could give

you your youth back or some truth
good enough to take its place, erase
recollections of lost balls and days.
The songs we sang as we traveled
along and on are lost to us too

We must summon new bravery as we
take up new games. I can not find and
give your missing baseball back to you
any more than I am able to map out
the road you took from field to far afield.

But there is something I have been
making for you; a ball you can hold and
wind and throw from this day on. Take it
along to wherever you go and know

it is given with all the love I had for it
while I had it. Only a ball, round, small,
not your ball of old but yours now to
play with, or if you should choose
hit over the fence, or tent and lose.

Daylily Blossoms
for Frances Gatlin

Borning
in the middle night
opening at dawn.
A single day
    of brilliant bloom
then slipping, aging, gone.

Ah, but what a perfect life,
a metaphor for lives
    of every kind;
busy morning,
    shining mid-day,
        languid afternoon.
Then pollen swollen sunset
deepening into darkness
    and the ever after.

Daylily blossoms
    dancing out
across a thousand Junes
is all the proof
    we need of God,
and Nature singing
    his own songs,
his rumble-tumble tunes.

Roundabout

Every day we live life to the fullest
we die a little but who complains?
Not the man who props his pocket
open to catch an extra share
of unexpected rain. Not the woman,
love exhausted, told by her lover
that she has never been more
beautiful than those few minutes
lying there half smiling like the
softest breeze that rattles gentle
leaves at the tops of tallest trees.
Not the child who after school
was knocked half-winded to the ground
by a fly ball in a favorite game.

Every day we hold on to life as much
as the living can as we die a little more
inside and out. What a little price to pay
for entering the game of called roundabout.

A Crock of Flowers

A crock of flowers on the desk,
four days old begin to die.
No incantations murmured
            at their passing.

Left at the roadside as refuse
they become prized widow's weeds,
as one old woman scratches amid
the faded and still fading castaway
                    bouquet.

She finds three daisies, a dahlia,
a double sprig of lemon leaves
to brighten for a few more days
an empty coffee can that decorates
a cluttered table.

Even as she walks from sight
she starts arranging her new
floral masterpiece and passing past
a garden breaks a branch of lilac
to complete her scavenged
arrangement.

Downloading the Classics
for Marilyn Horne

Some Sopranos

for Brown Meggs

(Some sopranos have resonance where their brains should be.
Anna Russell)

Some sopranos stick to Strauss
Four Last Songs or Arabella
and when they reach September
since Strauss is all they've ever learned
it's all that they remember.

Some sopranos live in Connecticut
        some in Beverly Hills
others are doomed to live forever
in the shadow of Beverly Sills.

Some sopranos are past their prime
alas, before they reach it.
A diva's a diva cause God says so
not because someone can teach it.

Some sopranos, essaying Carmen
successfully compete with firehouse siren,
others are merely high strung,
it's all of those E's above C they've sung.

Some sopranos have such a claque
yelling Brava, Bravissimo, Bravo
they use a computer just to keep track
of payoffs for each perfect salvo.

Some sopranos get praised by critics
and it doesn't go to their head,
simply because acclaim doesn't come
till twenty years after they're dead.

Some sopranos doing Beethoven's Ninth
carry a Seagram's fifth,
it's then the Ode to Joy becomes
more a rift than a riff.

Some sopranos top the chart
with airs by Porter, not Mozart.

Some sopranos, built like pianos
are Brunnhildes from the start,
they bust up the scenery, muddy the Rhine
and pass it all off as high art.

Some sopranos sing from the head
more often than from the chest,
of such sopranos it's often said
"Why doesn't she give it a rest?"

Some sopranos lose rich Greeks
to the widows of presidents -
these are the ones light on brains
but heavy on resonance.

Castrati
for Richard Carlson

Giovanni Battista Velluti (1781 - 1861) One of the last male sopranos. Senor Velluti was celebrated throughout Europe for managing, because he had been caste rated early in life, to reach notes few men or women dared attempt.

Don't pity the lad selected to be
lad forever and ever
that snip of a boy whatever age he
is no less a man or less clever
than those who succumb
to the hot breath of lust
and when called to come
go sprinkle their dust
on the coals of the bed of desire.

So save all your tears
for yon boy soprano
who though old in years
only played with piano,
and resist if you can
bad jokes ala tutti and frutti,
all kinds of men make up species, man
Casanova as well as Velluti.

Madame Butterfly

for Flicka

Fast food comes to Japan

Where will I go, she said to her friend
now that the night draws nigh.
Am I ever to know his shoulder again
under the Japanese sky?

The horizon's as narrow as narrow can be,
it's naught but a long thin line
sitting here looking for ships on the sea
is worse than a watch on the Rhine.

Suzuki replied,
be brave Cho-Cho-san
and shake off those snivels and shivers
so Pinkerton lied
why not call Pizza Man
you can be sure he delivers.

La Boheme

for Christine Brewer

If only Mimi had seen "The Sound of Music,"

Whenever I feel the least bit upset
I let out a gentle cough,
the vapors ain't got me and won't get me yet
I'm just feeling a teensy bit off.
A fever's no reason to fret,
give in to pneumonia,
the doctor will own ya
and start diggin' your trough.

So wheeze when you're weary
harrumph when you're dreary
and sneeze if you please but don't frown.
Don't make the assumption
you've got consumption,
you may be out but not down.

Carmen

for Suzanna Guzman

The reign in Spain is over now
Juan Carlos has been buried.
Suddenly it's whoa, not wow
and life's a bit more varied.
The Don Jose, once young and gay
is older now and married.
Two or three more years wasted away
aren't you sorry you tarried?

Monarchy destroyed, troops deployed
camp followers must now break camp,
pull down the tent, douse the lamp,
Democracy will thrive
a bit disarmin', Madame Carmen,
but at least you're still alive.

Ludwig Answers his Critics   for Billy Joel

Moonlight Sonata. The nickname of Beethoven's Sonata in C# minor, Op. 27, No. 2, not titled by the composer, but probably due to a description of the first movement by Rellstab. It does not fit the other two movements in the least.

Had I wanted to write
a lunar sonata
I'd have kept the left hand
playing triplets with spirit
like da-da-da, da-da-da
da-da-da, dot, dot, dotta.
A bit boring perhaps
to some of you chaps
but I wouldn't have had
     to hear it.

American Strand
for Chuck Ashman

American Strand

A wondrous thing it is to have
      a country you can love,
a field to lie with,
hill to hike,
a patch of woods so honorable
it stands as its own creed.
Cities too within the land
that belch and puff and bubble up
mixing native / foreign colors
        of its people,
each contributing.

It is a healthy wondrous thing
to have a country you can love.

He who loves his country first has
time for children and for walking,
talking in his sleep, rolling down a hill,
and finding one who supersedes all
                  other loves.

Time will take the patriot on an endless
journey and it will seem like overnight.
His list of pursuits can challenge
The new math and still his mind will stay
                              uncluttered.

If you would put yourself, your house
in order, try thinking of your country
first, and you will learn that order is
              the secret of selectivity.

Believe it. Try it, anyway.

It is a wondrous thing to have
              a country you can love

Courage

for Dan Rather

Courage rises up against
the darkest wave. It floats
and flies beyond the foam.
Part of the watermark of man
that includes in no special order,
kindness, strength, courtesy and
gentleness. It stays somewhere
between honesty and love. And is
no less a part of what we are or
should be than simplicity and
straightforwardness continue as
the hallmark of artistry and genius.

Not to be aware of courage in
others and the need for it within
your own daily life is to cheat
yourself or close yourself from truth.

Reality

It lies just over there.
No longer out of reach,
no longer separated
from what we thought it was.
We now know what it is
and how to call it
    what it is.

For years
whole lifetimes, maybe
we passed it off as boredom.
It is only now we recognize it
by its real name. Peace.

Riders to the Stars

How delicate is the way back home
                    from heaven.

They dream the bigger dreams, and why
because they feel that worlds exist
beyond what we call sky.

To mingle with the moons and stars
and wade the Milky Way and see
The Earth as little more
than distant scenery passing by.

Air Force Lt. Col. Michael P. Anderson,
Navy Capt. David A Brown, Kalpana
Chawla, Navy Cmdr. Laurel Clark,
Air Force Col. Rick D Husband,
Navy Cmdr. William C. McCool,
Israeli Air Force Col. Ilan Ramon.

Iowa From an Airplane

Above Iowa and looking down
the patchwork quilt of farms
unfolding through the oval window.
Now short green squares,
now broad gray triangles
and oblong stretches
of fresh-turned chocolate earth
that surveyors would find hard
          to pace off.
Pilots and pleats of land
orphaned from a quilting bee.

Though mid April grapples
with the middle earth, bare
trees still stand bare. Airports
are the only eyesore as silos dot
and red barns dash the land,
and God plays bridge with
unseen friends and shows the world
                    His hand.

Tractors track the squares
and fences follow every crooked
line they helped create, though
even fences make no boundary lines
and Iowa in the eye seems full enough
to spill across the continent if not
 across the world.

That was Then

for Matt

Elko Winter, 1946

The animals are filing down the fences
in a row heading back toward the barn,
though just let out to pasture
even they know this winter will be long.
Cold has not yet threatened them,
but they sense that first snow
                           is only hours away.
Sometimes a cow will start surefooted,
then slide down the banks of an irrigation
ditch to break the thin ice for a drink.
no more than just a chilly taste of winter.

Sheep are bleating just to bleat. Goat tails
wiggle at imaginary flies as energetically
as they protest the fly-infested summers.
A habit. I have a habit too unbroken
since I came here years ago. Long after
sunset, the cows milked, the barn door locked,
the gate closed and the porch light dimmed
I lie awake and listen for the trains.

This year again I have the same old, unfilled Christmas wish, to ride away some night on an southbound train and never see the barnyard, the east field or feel the snow again.

I will be warm one day. I will. One day there will be an absence of winter.

San Francisco, 1953

Always the outsider,
    me and them.

The night is made of
too many properties
to put down in words.

Throngs milling on Market
a gang fight on the corner
a masquerade in every bar
lovers stomachless in parked cars.

Tonight it is not confetti
or serpentine flying
or a masquerade remembered,
only another eye to eye held
by another sloe-eyed stranger.

Tagu, Korea 1955

The tall soldier's helmet
gleaming in the sun
he stands apart a little
               from the rest,
a vanguard in the narrow street
between the rows of barracks.
Passing past each other our
awkward stares lock a minute
in challenge, or recognition?

Were you expecting? I half
expected you although I could
not divine the time of day
you might arrive, I perceived
               your coming.

Now? Truce perhaps and only
later trust. And if later does
not come there was that instant
of challenge or concern. I will
always choose to remember it
               as recognition.

Where do the eagles go in winter,
do the big birds hibernate like bears
or is this yet another secret I am not
                supposed to know?
Three winter questions in a single
sentence on a summer day
with no answers coming and if they did
                from where?

A jeep chugs by and kicks dust into
                a little whirlwind
that dances down the road.
I still have to make it through another
Autumn before a furlough home.

The Yellow Unicorn, New York 1959

This morning I woke up just in time to see
a yellow unicorn eating the low branches
from the linden tree outside. Then
into the green he ran and was gone.

Alone now again with sunlight
the color of the unicorn moving over the wall
and low clouds and the hot July of New York
about me, I think about Diamante's green eyes,
or maybe the one called Dov, or others.

Some I loved whose arms and names
I never knew. The girl in Peter's bar, or
                          a face on the train;
Mostly in the last year I have felt this kind
of love. Mostly being away from home
forgetting the Summer Park and special rooms
                          did this to me.

And one night hearing a big woman say
as she was stroking my head I wish there
had been someone like you
                         when I was young.
I went away and began to love strangers,
people I would see only once on buses
and in bars or walking by themselves
                         in quiet places.

And in this last year there must have been
a hundred who never knew a funny little boy
watched them and loved them.

It has taken me a long time to learn
                         while I'm in bars
not to tear the label from my beer bottle.
A girl once told me it makes me
look too neurotic and to get the people
I want it works best to be boyish.

So, I am a little boy
growing older, true, but a little boy
who still sees unicorns and still believes
in love and lies best when the girl
who is making love to him lies too.

It's okay to tell people nice things
when the lights are out, after the act
is over and you are close.

Even if sometimes the things you say
aren't true. It's okay because they forget
about it when the next big guy comes along.
And anyway, maybe you mean them
                              at the time.
Not maybe. I believe I do.

It is hard to put your arms around
someone, even for a minute, if you
are not a little bit in love with them.

People like to be told nice things. But how
can you let someone know that all you really
want in life is to lie close in someone's
shadow without words or even promises
                              just being close.

Look... there goes the unicorn.

The Coming of the Rain, Paris 1967

Where were we
when the coming of the rain
made us turn from conversation to the window?

In mustard fields maybe,
 or the love jungle, and
as we talked
we were with others, not ourselves.

I was thinking of old birthdays and holidays
gone wrong, pretty people seen on streetcars
 but never met.
Selling soda bottles to pay for movie matinees.
 I was twelve.
Tarzan was the man I most resembled
in those days. How can I have grown
so old without once swinging on a vine?

Did you think of party dresses
and high school plays or hallways
full of lovers yet to come?

The mind is such a junkyard; it remembers
candy bars but not the Gettysburg
Address,
Frank Sinatra's middle name but not the day
            your best friend died.

If in your head there is some corner
not yet occupied with numbers you may
never need, remind your memory of
the day we turned to watch the rain
and turning back forgot
that we belonged to one another.

From a Moscow Notebook, April 1978

North From Moscow, on the road to Susdal
more ravens than I have ever seen, gather
on Birch and pair off on Willow trees.

Spring tries hard to make a breakthrough.
Snow fences having done their job sag idle
        as white ice still forgets to melt.
Ponds are frosted, awaiting sun to free them.

Another church
and now another with golden domes
and silver spires that slice the sky,
Everywhere more naked trees, the crows nests
numerous as leaves in summer, embellish
                        their skeletons.

An ancient graveyard overlooks a sporting
field and every rural house is gingerbread.

Another church survives despite
the decades of banned worship it looks
lived in. We watch sparrows and barn
swallows dart inside the cracks of fading
green and copper colored domes.

Three joggers suited up in cobalt blue
are moving through a flock of geese
they cause goose giggles and a scattering
of plumage. No cattle, but the hay's been
freshly spread. The People's Power Plant
#201 momentarily ruins the landscape,
        we drive on.

Vladimir, another unmapped town
where factories and farmyards meet.
We are on The Road of Sorrows, a left
hand turn and now we glide along
      The Worker's Highway.

I suggest that when we sight another
church we stop this time and go inside.
We do. Our party minder and the driver
lag behind. We enter a cathedral
mid-restoration, newly painted icons nearly
blind us. We fill a widows hand with Kopeks
and purchase leaden crosses and ancient
icons - made in the rectory yesterday,
                              I suspect.

Ahead, mid church, and guarded by near volley
of votary, again their uniform is a widow black,
another unknown soldier's tomb. Our curiosity
and awe gives way to reverence and respect.
          I light a candle, kneel and pray
our Party Keeper is at the door.

How did what Russians term The Great
Patriotic War leave anyone but widows?
And yet sons, for sons to come have nearly
finished building second cities to supplant
                         those long gone.
One of our party observes; the countryside
could use a few less hod carriers
                and a lot more architects.

Prefabricated factories sprout from
requisitioned playgrounds, the roads
to each are lined with color-gone-mad
billboards stressing and addressing stress.
The People's enemy if each citizen still
expects his share of what The Motherland
                      goes on promising.

More murals with hard-jawed muscle men
in coveralls cover all the outside walls of
every factory. Each man more studly and
more handsome than the last. Then, dare
I say it - in a democratic bid, a random
fresco of a darling woman, strong but
comely, augments the paint by numbers
features of the not so common man.

Mother Russia, your people, mine,
not so unalike, each coming to worship
smiling white-teethed women, two fisted,
muscled, well hung men assaulting us from
roadsides, turnpikes, thoroughfares,
                      thorough fairs.

Our heroes all 'light up' imploring us to do the same. Yours exhort each worker to thrust his shoulder to the wheel of progress. The Marlboro-Salem Man, the exaggerated portrait of The Comrad, interchangeable. Each assures that by following the true religion we too can bulge where it counts, be colorful instead of dreary black & white.

That Was Then

What measure did I use
for counting days when I was twelve ·
holiday to holiday, allowance to allowance,
but no allowances were given
         none taken or expected·
I know some who tell time not by clocks
but by the frequency of hope rejected·
At twelve I had not learned
the meaning of such catchall words
as rejection or approval· I worked
for neither and neither bore me witness
or clocked the seasons passage·

I lived inside the five-and-dime where
wonder heaped on wonder could be had
for half a buck, or nothing when
the saleslady's back was turned·
The seasons changed for me
as merchandise went from paddle balls,
wax jack o' lanterns to Christmas balls·
Heart boxes then replaced lead tinsel·

Bullies vied for my attention then
like as not they rolled dice for the
privilege of my ambush after school.

The sissy trapping bees
inside tall hollyhock did not belong
in their world, any world. I became
the artful dodger, swift of foot,
curling deeper inward. Sensing I was
different but believing that my differences
were not special I harbored conflict
as a good companion.

Mirrors are too close to reflect change
while it is happening. Only later does
the young heart welcomes harvest time
                            as easily as spring.

Expectations are a trap
               as surely as the flame
so I stayed open for surprise and I was
never disappointed, not at nine or twelve
                     or two years later.

Without a list of what life owes you
to hold up as evidence, or lack of,
what comes is greeted with relief.
No banks failed for me because
I was not bankable. I gave and
I received as is the way of things
More doors opened than were closed.

This is Now-

for Margaret Whiting

This Is Now

for John Scoggins

The years pile up like cordwood
as sunsets stretch to dawn
and what is gone was no doubt
never here. And if it was
a never was then what is there
to muddle over and be sorry for?

What changes as the years roll on,
the time between never and forever,
the give and take of days, loss,
the depth and breadth of pain.
Sorrow has one hundred shades
and each of us is better for
having and sharing a measure of it

Joy and wisdom, the chance to learn
have higher peaks each day, each year
and loving someone without holding back
is the highest high of all.

White hair and age have no premium
and no disadvantage. They are what they are.

The bliss of small things and what is left
to chance continues as reward supreme
though life without remuneration or
a ribbon is plenty good enough. Tomorrow
is a victory by just arriving.

Never ask too much of anything,
but be willing to chance everything.

Still Life After All These Years

How is it now at a quarter past three
difficult, lovely, painful, good.
The moon on the lake is especially nice
    in middle age or otherwise.
All of the intervals meeting at once,
those in music, those in time, those
that cross and meld in the mind. Coming
together staying apart, lost in diversions
                              dancing starts.

Friends remembered, new friends made,
companions dependable whatever the hour.
Not every dream fulfilled,
        but not every dream considered.
Always some new door opening the same
        day an old one closes.
Mama buried all these years
and still her bushes throw off new roses.

Ever the romantic believing love
the brick, the mortar, building block.
Handel discovered, Mozart renewed.
Mahler and Bartok at last understood.,

And what of the fires that blaze awhile
and then go out without mystery -
is there regret, a shrug of resign,
bafflement at lack of warning,
        a cry, UNFAIR?
All the above and more.
Bewilderment. Betrayal.
        Self-hate swarming.

But, there are the travels
through difficult books,
    unfriendly lands,
torment at the hands of experts
with a last minute fall into grace.

However thick the mind gets
with thickets, there is always
a clearing, a twang of birds,
        a black leopard cat
on his way home from Zion
who'll give you a ride on his back.
Still one more season to crawl through.
Still one more Alice-hole-in-the-wall
        to fall through.

And always and ever au suivant.
The next and the next, and the next
                              after that.

Indelible impressions, like digital tape,
some of the soul is missing but most
things clear and in shape. Sighs, not
breezes, songs unlike wind. Nothing
coming easily, everything redefined,
                              hour by hour.

If there is a creed floating over it all,
this nonsense and stuff to be gotten
through, it's some kind of love
into everything. Some kind of selflessness
out of self. A kernel of truth distilled
                              from the lie.

If someone rocks the cradle be glad
it is not the ark. If someone falls
and will not rise run to help him up.

Because I cannot fill every want
my needs are more. My desires
greater each time out. But I have
nothing any more I would not exchange,
                              or give away,
for a little more talent, a little more time,
                    a wider sense of focus.
Focus is the juncture
where it all begins to unravel.

Legend says that the drunken Li Po
tried to reach and grasp and hold
the moon's reflection. Alas, he lost
his balance, fell overboard
                    and drowned.

Any poet worth his word will tell you
the moon on the lake is especially nice
but always dangerous
           in middle age or otherwise.

I Always Knew

I always knew
that you would find me;
no clock needed as reminder
that it would happen.
I planned on it, worked it out,
hid in plain sight every day
knowing you would pass,
that way or this, come along,
go by, pause in moving to
here or somewhere; near or
far it did not matter. You
              would arrive.
It kept the heart
alive and thriving in the clatter
of time's travel to know
that you would turn and see me,
then not turn away. You here
or coming, unraveling the puzzle,
kept me whole and safe
and driving on toward this day.

When the evenings, like forever,
started fleeting, going fast,
I could see you at some distance
disappearing in the mist.
In the mass of fondled faces
one imagines in a lifetime
yours was there just out of grasp.

As you fluttered in my future,
fled throughout my lifelong past,
I expected every spring to bring you
to my arms, to my side. When
the autumns started coming thick
and firm and fast, I never once
gave up believing you'd arrive
with winter's passing; you would
be here as the moon fell.

As the sun rose we would clasp
hands at first, then bodies closing
up that awful gap that life without
a lifelong partner leaves between
the noon and nightline.

Did I falter in my faith? Once
or twice perhaps, but never long
enough to leave you languishing in
some dream that wasn't mine.
Because I always knew that you
Would find me, I never sent out
Distress signals, never tapped out
SOS. I was blessed
with growing knowledge. Something
whispered, do not worry; it will
happen; it's been planned. Nothing
here is happenstance. Do not hurry.
Do not pause to catch your breath.
So it was I always knew.

Now and then I leapt to heaven
on another's stroke or kiss, lent
to me to keep me going in this
sure direction. Afterward the same
affection that I saved, assigned to you,
only grew. I always knew that you
would find me and so I did not
bother scrawling each and every
new address on cloud or curbstone.
Why? I was waiting; you knew the rest.

A nocturne for the King of Naples,
          and one for Edmond White.
A serenade or two for those who
got me through some fearful midnights.
Sonatas for some faces time erases but
does not forget. A double wind concerto
for the wind itself; it could have blown
me anywhere but wouldn't, didn't. I
dropped some songs along the way in
laps of strangers, even laps I knew. But
this music you see spread around you,
these notes and half notes, planted long
ago, that grew and grew were saved,
because I always knew that you would
find me and help me with the harvest.

The strongholds, the havens that
proved weak and wanting, lessons
learned, prizes earned, not always
given. Paths I paved, paths unpaved.
The rest of what I have to offer, little
things this life has amassed, for you.
For you. It was for you I saved
the best for last.

The Poet Caught Mid Song

I should be writing reams of velvet
and not so velvet verse. But this is Sunday,
The Muse, The Cats are fast asleep.

I should be staking claims on sentences
and stocking up on verbs against the time
of feeble mind and end of energy to come.

I know you, Lack Of Inspiration, by whatever
guise or name you've chosen or will choose.
                                            Age, Apathy,
or high-falutin' nom de plume like
No One To Motivate The Old Man Anymore.

When you were friendlier, not given to
disguise, and I was younger than the moon
was and twice as quick to rise I used to write
about you all the time. And rhyme you too.

Don't you recall all the fond remembering I did
back then about some week old romance, day old
kiss, handshake half an hour past, as if the long
ago was measured by the second hand and not
                                            the hourglass.

All those look back songs, reflective airs when neon and nostalgia both were tame. When love was such a lofty thing and tangling in legs and arms was all the height one needed to attain.

Youth was ever naked in the night and always innocent. Delight had no restrictions and no pain. Spring hung heavy even when it was not there.

Way back when God did not damn the rain. Love was brief but longed for, always getting up and going home. But ever coming back in brand new shifts and trousers. Coming back and coming back again, as love will do no matter where it's been. We was used by linguists to mean two, and not the cosmos. And it was never me and you against the universe. You were pretty. I was wise. We were comatose and pleased to be so.

I remember what some memories cost before the table was upended and the lot was lost, the price is always cheep enough when the prize is ripe.

I dare not tell myself, let alone the world how
satisfied I am with life right now. Brag about
contentment and its sure to bite you in the ass.

I should be busy now constructing songs and
Sonnets for the fortress. Else I'll never get
through silly, chilly nights of second childhood
when it comes. When the hand becomes unable
to navigate the prized machine and fingertips
fail to tease the keyboard all I'll have to play with
is my mind.

I scribble little bits, enough to satisfy a thirsty
Journal on most nights, but not enough to give
Ned Rorem pause or cause for second Seconals.
The trunk has an excess of started but unfinished
tunes. Some will wait till not at all for a lyric
promised on some boozy nineteen sixties night. Many
are bare-boned because the cannibal poet needed
one
more line for one more abandoned, thus unpublished
song.

In the note books there are parts of poems, pieces
of prose that rest on unresolved, I have no desire
to
disturb their sweet slumber. And anyway, some odes
will not rise up in the morning and cooperate no
matter
how you treat or entreat them.

Hymns there are to him and her, hearts forgotten or that were not. The promise gone, the passion never. My ardor for all that catches my attention is as eager
as it ever was to be wrenched from me and quenched.

I am informed that JA has finished a single poem of one hundred pages. Could he have heard Macarthur saying I Shall Return? The news has sent Mc back to his MAC.

Old soldiers never die, or shouldn't without a few unpublished manuscripts stuffed in books or mashed in mattresses to pay off unexpected taxes, help defray the hangman's debt and buy the gang a wake.

I am not cheered by friends who quote the histories of old composers pumping out their prime only after humping middle age? Who knows what middle is until he's seen both ends.

It would not make the music better if I knew that I was working on my own unfinished air. These days every whole note's hard to part with, the left hand rests grow longer. Some sonatas come without legato, magically measured, others stall at pencil breaks.

The heart that beats the rhythm and the head that
marks the time have forgotten how to take their naps
in consort. I should be penning preludes to ward the
calm a-coming. Instead I choose to drift back to
that time when I was happy drifting.

Still, today, this mid November Sunday with its
indecision, rambling back and forward, wasn't bad.
Could be the middle gear is much abused by word
of mouth but not by seasoned drivers.

I always did enjoy the intervals the most, using
the space between the words or notes to say
those things most needed to be said.

The hesitation just before the strings come in is
still my favorite mid-song time. And my, I've had
some lovely, lofty high string lines.

Instead of all this rambling I should be doing IT.

A Better Place
for David Galligan

The Possible

for Patrick Mace

If you can dream it you can do it
      I know that to be true.
We have no dreams so lofty
That we cannot stand on tiptoe
and pick ourselves a few.

Our nightmares, and we all share
         our share
are not so filled with mavericks
that a little sunlight cannot
send them back to those
dark corners where they leer
and lurk and stir their kettles
      and their cauldrons.
Bullies frighten big and small ones
but give a though to it,
do you know anyone who died
of fright from something that
went bumping, thumping through
some dreary night? Exactly.

If you want it you can earn it
          Need a sentence
to write home about?
Study hard and learn it.

There's a way 'round everything.
Anything you dream about
has a door that you can open
          and go through.

Look at me I'm sitting here
spending time with you.

High Heavens There Are

High heavens there are low
heavens too and as many
in between as there are
clouds to populate the ones
                    we know.

I watch. I wait. Not for
any path to open up that
point to heavens near or far,
but for something.

Something isn't always
very much but more often
than not it is more than nothing.

Don't Imagine Endings

It does not end here.
Here being where you are
or where you go and go again.
Not even where you think you might
be heading if you had that roadmap
every preacher promises.

Please do not read belief
especially my belief as mysticism.
It is only that I know you cannot
work and wonder and go on working
and pass along all wrinkles on the outside
with Technicolor of what might have been
still merry making and blowing whistles
 inside of you.

No tricks or treats or magic produce
a heaven or a proper hell. And haven't
you had hell enough already and maybe
 just a whiff or two of heaven?
That ought to do you.

2.
Borrow? Yes. Give back? If your conscience
catches you in time and I hope it does.

Keep? Not since they peopled pyramids
with bandaged bodies soaked in henna
leaves and oil has one among us slipped away
and taken with them anything of value.
But something's out there, if not on platforms
            or a cloud, somewhere, somewhere.

Why not believe? The cost is negligible.
The truth of anything not known, but certainly
supposed is not quite as sure as anything
we know. What are we sure of? Nothing
anyone has yet been able to prove
                        and if so, improve upon.

Go to sleep with ease, for hours or forever
as far as anybody knows it could or could not be
your first step into heaven or the last you take
                    leading from forever.
Why not wait and be surprised.

Circles & Squares   for Ben McMillan

When someone's whistle fades
take up the song. Embrace the tune,
pass it 'round until it's strong enough
to go off on its own.

If someone stumbles in the ring
it does not mean the fight is done,
perhaps it indicates this match
may have to go another round.

Instead of worrying about defeat,
retreat a little then go back.
It does not take magicianship
to get ahead, you only need walk on.

Earthling

for Mario Spanicciati

None of us will ever be
as rich as the earth we walk upon,
as precious as the space we occupy,
as important as the time we waste
           that cannot be bought back.

And we can never be as noble
           as a blade of grass
or as smooth as clouds
we swallow and piss out, unaware.

What we can be are teachers while
We learn, gentle men and ladies
to our friends, faithful lovers to
those we love, good citizens
           to our country.

Do not expect to be remembered
past your usefulness, too many
live, too many die, life in passing
is just that. Be effective while you
are here. That is the loftiest, only
           reason for being.

A Few of Us Will Still Stay On

Angels hover in the alcoves of the stone cathedral
disguised as choirs of children. Old women,
black shoes and stockings graduating to black dresses
and the midnight hood send time backward in a
bounce.

Long silences well meant to stretch a conversation
sever it instead as we go back to rooms and lofts
long corridors of nothingness, great bushels full of
nowhere, armloads of emptiness.

Has reason lost its spokes and hub? Believing
fantasy to be the only highway into life I arise and
go
into the street attempting to erase reality whatever
its disguise. Like the nag who knows the curve
of every track I am soon back at the starting gate
or heading for the barn.

I set out all my candles and leave them burning
in the wind. Not content to fire a bridge or two
I dynamite the dams and drain the rivers. I waste
not time by buying time, I squander it by always
reaching far beyond my grasp. I have insured myself
against memory and being remembered.

Some of us who know that we are fragments
do not even wish to be the whole. only part of
something larger, satellites to something.

If promises were guarantees I would by now
have given half my life away and owned a half
I will not know.

The sense of solitude is that it makes no sense.
It is not condition or religion but so of itself
to be beyond description. It is as pure as
unadulterated green and clean as seas unsighted.

I am on the cusp of something. And who of us is not? Tension drags like drops of silver in the air. It is everywhere. Some will surrender long before the liberating troops arrive without the truth as armor they will wither, others may get halfway down the block before dementia or boredom traps them in an alleyway.

A few of us will stay on till the end and be rewarded with whatever endings are. Here for the long haul, I am not impatient, only weary of an afternoon when progress has not taken up and carried on its shoulder the flag of pride.

Caveat

for Bruce Bellingham

Never mind the joints that ache
the bones more brittle
        than they were at twenty.

The memory lapses
and the end resembling the beginning
as we toddle much like toddlers,
into age and then beyond
        all of it part of the ride.

From that first slap alive we travel
on deaths road. Life like everything
has a beginning, a middle and an end.
Wherever you may think you are
        on that chain,
surprises cannot be avoided.

I promise you that growing older
in all ways but one is safe and
easy, something to be savored.

The downside? Outliving friends
that cannot be replaced, those
few that always make and made
                    a difference.

Ride on.
Live for those who did not complete
the journey, make a difference
            for them.

Index to First Lines

A crock of flowers on the desk   92
A health to everything that's new   70
A wondrous thing it is to have a country you can love   105
A young man standing in the rain outside   68
Above Iowa and looking down   110
Always the stranger   117
Angels hover in the alcoves of the stone cathedral   160
August has been halved. The warm part done   51
Beach bar lingo being all the same   57
Borning in the middle night opening at dawn   90
Courage rises up against the darkest wave   107
Dawn is the decider. Not just of night   23
Discarded. Given up.   83
Don't pity the lad expected to be   98
Every day we live life to the fullest   91
Goodbye is a word that should be used only   64
Had I wanted to write a lunar sonata   102
He had hoped that even as an older tree   15
High heavens there are low heavens too   155
How delicate is the way back home from heaven   109
How fragile are the dreams that cross and meet   61
How good it feels to concentrate on others   73
How is it now at a quarter past three?   137
I always knew that you would find me   141
I am content to count the cobblestones   21
I am the blade that slices the rose   25
I do not have to be with you to have high spirits   53
I enter you, rest awhile, the darkness here is safe   41
I hold in wonder the wonders of the day   38
I light one candle with another's flame   59
I like my body lying next to yours   42
I never saved your letters though I wish I had   35

I should be writing reams of velvet and not so velvet verse.   145
I walked home through the field alone   53
I watch you slowly turning gold   58
I wish I could give back to you   87
If one thousand men walking through this world   78
If you can dream it you can do it   153
In certain cities you will find   75
It does not end here   156
It lies just over there.   108
Love winds down as does the day   18
Never mind the joints that ache   163
No ordinary moons orbit in August   48
None of us will ever be as rich as the earth we walk upon   159
North from Moscow on the Road to Susdal   125
Now slowly like a muffled drum   47
Snow has now begun to comb her hair   86
Some sopranos stick to Strauss   95
The animals are filing down the fences   115
The full moon, buzz saw-like now   50
The Melody Begins   45
The old oak stands almost alone   29
The reign in Spain is over now   101
The space between us now is greater than   20
The tall soldier's helmet gleaming in the sun   118
The years pile up like cordwood   135
This morning I woke up just in time to see   120
Tis a good job Warren does not have a garden   76
Was ever a bed so long awaited   66
What measure did I use for counting days   130
When someone's whistle fades   158
When valentines are obsolete   65
Whenever I feel the least bit upset   100
Where were we when the coming of the rain   123
Where will I go she said to her friend   99
With the morning's early breath   27

About the Author

ROD McKUEN's books of poetry, numbering more than 60 titles, have been translated into 30 languages and have made him the best-selling, most widely read poet of his time. The publication of Rusting in the Rain marks the 50th Anniversary of his first 1st book "and autumn came". His first attention as a poet came in the early fifties, when he read with Kerouac and Ginsburg at San Francisco's Jazz Cellar. Working with Jazz artists such as Stan Getz, and Chet Baker at that time greatly influenced his early songwriting.

As a songwriter McKuen's familiar standards include "Love's Been Good To Me", "Jean", "I Think of You", "Rock Gently", "I've Been to Town," "The World I Used To Know", 'Champion Charlie Brown', 'Joanna' 'The Importance of the Rose' and "I'll Catch The Sun". His 17-year collaboration with Jacques Brel that he terms equal parts translation, adaptation and collaboration produced "Seasons in the Sun," "If You Go Away," "I'm Not Afraid," "The Port of Amsterdam," "To You," "The Far West" and dozens of other songs.

Perry Como, Petula Clark, Madonna, Johnny Cash, Pete Fountain, Andy Williams, The Kingston Trio, Percy Faith, Tom Jones, The London Philharmonic, Johnny Cash, Dusty Springfield, Janet Jackson, Johnny Mathis, Shirley Bassey, Waylon Jennings and Frank Sinatra are among the eclectic entertainers who have recorded and performed his songs. Sinatra commissioned an entire album of original McKuen songs resulting in the highly successful and acclaimed "A Man Alone," It produced two hit singles for Sinatra and later became the inspiration for Nina Simone's final album.

The composers' film music has twice been nominated for Academy Awards (The Prime of Miss Jean Brodie & A Boy Named Charlie Brown). His classical works (symphonies, concertos, suites, chamber music and song cycles) are performed by leading orchestras and concert artists. "The City," a suite he composed for Narrator & Orchestra, was nominated for a Pulitzer Prize in Music. He has received commissions for classical work from The Royal Philharmonic, The Louisville Orchestral, Edmonton Symphony and National Symphony.

McKuen's own recordings, including more than 40 gold and platinum titles, have sold in excess of 200 million copies worldwide. He has been nominated for 7 Grammy's and won for best-spoken word album, "Lonesome Cities." As a performer he regularly plays the major international concert halls and venues. In 2003 he appeared for the 24th time at New York's Carnegie Hall in what was billed as "The 30th Anniversary of his 40th Birthday Concert."

Since1998 he has had a web site;" Rod McKuen / A Safe Place To Land" - www.mckuen.com. In addition to poetry, music, photographs and personal information the author contributes a column to the site entitled "Flight Plan." In the past 6 years it has become one of the Internet's most visited personal sites and spawned a mirror site www. rodmckuen.com to handle the volume of daily 'hits'. Stanyan, the innovative record & publishing company he founded in the 1960's recently opened www.stanyanhouse.com to handle mail order, licensing & merchandising of its extensive copyright and master recording catalogue.

Between concert and benefit appearances McKuen is currently

completing two-dozen songs he began writing with Johnny Mercer that remained unfinished during the famed lyricist's lifetime and he is finishing a series of compositions in various stages of development he began with his friend the late Jacques Brel. "If it wasn't for Margaret Whiting," he says. "The Mercer songs would still be in the trunk and God knows when I'd have gotten back to the Brel-McKuen stuff ."

It is not unusual for the compulsive and prolific McKuen to put in a series of 18-hour working days to complete a project, "crash-sleep" for a few days and then begin the same process again. "I work for the absolute fun of it and to please others," McKuen said recently, "long ago I stopped trying to satisfy myself."

McKuen hopes to complete his next book, "A Soldier of the Heart", in time for publication in early 2005. That year he will he will again appear at Carnegie Hall as part of a gala honoring the centenary of Harold Arlen.

For the past 34 years the author has made his home in Southern California where he lives with his brother and partner Edward and a pride of cats, Dinah, Rocky, Kubby Kat Too and Sunny.

A NOTE ON THE PRODUCTION OF THIS BOOK

Rusting in the Rain was produced in its entirety on an HP Media Center PC integrated with a Macintosh PowerBook G4 computer using postScript software applications.

The typefaces are by P22 Type Foundry, Buffalo New York. Titles & Ornaments:
P22 Dard Hunter, Main body copy: P22 Stanyan Autumn & P22 Stanyan Autumn Bold, Headline & Cheval-Stanyan Logo: P22 Stanyan Eros, Copyright page, About the Author, index to first lines & this page: P22 Manuscripty.

Richard Kegler, head designer, typographer and proprietor of the P22 Type foundry, designed P22 Stanyan Autumn especially for this book. It is based on the noted artist Anthony Goldsmidt's calligraphy for the 1969 Edition of Rod McKuen's "... and autumn came." This marks the first use of it as well as the premiere of P22 Manuscripty

Book design: Rod McKuen, Jacket design: Richard Kegler

The completed manuscript was printed and bound in Miami, Florida by A&A Color, Inc.

HP is a registered trademark of Hewlett Packard Inc., Macintosh is a registered trademark of Apple Computers Inc., PostScript is a registered trademark of Adobe Systems Inc. & P22 is a registered trademark of P22 Type Foundry Inc.

ADDITIONAL SOURCES

The Yellow Unicorn is from the album of the same name, this is its first publication, copyright 1963 by Rod McKuen & Stanyan Music Group; Beach Bar Lingo is from Sea Cycle, copyright 1967 by Rod McKuen & Stanyan Music Group; The Coming of the Rain is from Listen to the Warm, copyright 1967 by Rod McKuen & Stanyan Music Group; Noon is from Seasons in the Sun, copyright 1974 by Rod McKuen & Stanyan Music Group; Through the Field is from We Touch the Sky, copyright 1979 by Rod McKuen & Stanyan Music Group; Don't Imagine Endings, Ourselves to Know & Winter People are from Love's Been Good to Me, copyright 1979 by Rod McKuen & Stanyan Music Group. All Rights Reserved

High Heavens There Are is from Alone, copyright 1975 by Rod McKuen & Stanyan Music Group; Iowa From Above is from An Outstretched Hand, copyright 1980 by Rod McKuen & Stanyan Music Group; Looking for a Friend & Night Mischief are from Looking for a Friend, copyright 1980 by Rod McKuen & Stanyan Music Group; Roundabout is from The Beautiful Strangers, copyright 1981 by Rod McKuen & Stanyan Music Group; Reality is from Too Many Midnights, copyright 1981 by Rod McKuen & Stanyan Music Group; After Hour Acrobatics, Holding On & Music Room are from The Sound of Solitude, copyright 1983 by Rod McKuen & Stanyan Music Group; Mid August & Sandbag are from Watch for the Wind, copyright 1983 by Rod McKuen & Stanyan Music Group. All Rights Reserved

America, Lillian at Fifty, Sacrament & The Truthful Lover are from Suspension Bridge, copyright 1984 by Rod McKuen & Stanyan Music Group; Still Life After all These Years is from Intervals, copyright 1986 by Rod McKuen & Stanyan Music Group; Nobody's Heart is from Valentines, copyright 1986 by Rod McKuen & Stanyan Music Group; Daylilies was written for and first appeared in Daylilies: The Beginner's Handbook, copyright 1991 by Rod McKuen & Stanyan Music Group; The Poet Caught Mid-Song first appeared in the album Speaking of Love, Copyright 1994 by Rod McKuen & Stanyan Music Group; Can We Have Our Ball Back was written for and first appeared on the website of the same name, copyright 2000 by Rod McKuen & Stanyan Music Group; I Always Knew is from A Safe Place to Land, copyright 2001 by Rod McKuen & Stanyan Music Group. All Rights Reserved.